Table of Contents

① 57
+ 41

② 34
+ 23

③ 6
+ 83

④ 27
+ 51

⑤ 30
+ 16

⑥ 92
+ 3

⑦ 12
+ 24

⑧ 46
+ 41

⑨ 75
+ 11

⑩ 28
+ 31

⑪ 5
+ 33

⑫ 56
+ 12

⑬ Marcia has 14 boys in her class and 12 girls. How many kids are in her class?

⑭ There are 51 second graders and 44 third graders. How many kids are in both grades combined?

⑮ At recess, there are 13 kids playing on the playground and 20 kids playing in the field. How many kids are there in all?

① 85
+ 1

② 43
+ 15

③ 22
+ 27

④ 3
+ 83

⑤ 14
+ 4

⑥ 37
+ 20

⑦ 61
+ 23

⑧ 25
+ 21

⑨ 53
+ 12

⑩ 5
+ 32

⑪ 18
+ 41

⑫ 64
+ 32

⑬ Gary's basketball team had 34 points at half time, then then they scored 22 more points in the second half. How many points did his team score all together?

⑭ Casey scored 12 points and Nathan scored 7 points. How many points did these two friends score together?

⑮ Kelly has 14 girls on her team. The other team has 13 girls. How many girls are on the two teams combined?

Name:_____ Date:_____

① 11
+ 13

② 17
+ 32

③ 42
+ 21

④ 55
+ 12

⑤ 34
+ 2

⑥ 8
+ 41

⑦ 20
+ 31

⑧ 64
+ 23

⑨ 10
+ 25

⑩ 52
+ 32

⑪ 44
+ 14

⑫ 1
+ 17

⑬ Sarah had 11 books checked out from the library, then she checked out 4 more. How many books does she have now?

⑭ The librarian bought 23 new books for the library last month and 32 new books this month. How many new books did he buy?

⑮ One of the bookcases has 42 books on the first shelf and 36 books on the second shelf. How many books are on this bookcase?

Name:_____ Date:_____

Score: /15

① 14
+ 21

② 32
+ 40

③ 25
+ 12

④   2
+ 23

⑤ 52
+ 7

⑥ 44
+ 10

⑦ 64
+ 15

⑧ 81
+ 3

⑨ 21
+ 27

⑩ 33
+ 5

⑪ 52
+ 24

⑫ 12
+ 6

⑬ The post office has 63 letters in one bag and 31 letters in another bag. How many letters are there?

⑭ A postal worker delivers mail to 45 homes on one street and 41 homes on another street. What is the total number of homes this worker delivered mail to?

⑮ Megan mailed 22 invitations for her party on Monday and 5 more on Tuesday. How many invitations did she send?

Name:_____ Date:_____

① 48
+ 36

② 53
+ 23

③ 77
+ 64

④ 39
+ 6

⑤ 81
+ 24

⑥ 15
+ 58

⑦ 34
+ 29

⑧ 42
+ 74

⑨ 36
+ 57

⑩ 18
+ 22

⑪ 93
+ 65

⑫ 60
+ 24

⑬ The zoo has 13 poisonous snakes and 39 that are nonpoisonous. How many snakes does the zoo have?

⑭ There were 17 monkeys in the trees and 28 on the ground. How many monkeys were there all together?

⑮ The zoo has 47 penguins swimming in the water and 26 napping on land. How many penguins are there?

Name:_____ Date:_____

① 9
+ 29

② 46
+ 82

③ 24
+ 67

④ 87
+ 72

⑤ 65
+ 12

⑥ 14
+ 81

⑦ 32
+ 28

⑧ 75
+ 64

⑨ 59
+ 52

⑩ 31
+ 86

⑪ 47
+ 93

⑫ 89
+ 13

⑬ Aubrey and Ethan went fishing for 25 minutes in the morning and 30 minutes in the evening. How much time did they spend fishing?

⑭ Aubrey caught 37 fish and Ethan caught 25 fish. How many fish did they catch together?

⑮ The fish ate 18 of Aubrey's worms and 23 of Ethan's worms. How many worms did the fish eat all together?

Name:_____ Date:_____

Score: /15

① 17
+ 34

② 83
+ 96

③ 52
+ 25

④ 18
+ 14

⑤ 67
+ 45

⑥ 11
+ 54

⑦ 66
+ 48

⑧ 92
+ 27

⑨ 63
+ 21

⑩ 8
+ 13

⑪ 50
+ 72

⑫ 61
+ 55

⑬ Noah found 15 starfish at the beach and Amelia found 26. How many did they find all together?

⑭ They saw two pods of dolphins. The first pod had 28 dolphins, the second pod had 16. How many dolphins did they see?

⑮ There were 63 people at the beach, then a group of 22 more people came. How many people were at the beach after that?

Name:_____ Date:_____

① 88
+ 97

② 64
+ 24

③ 37
+ 7

④ 81
+ 86

⑤ 58
+ 92

⑥ 33
+ 83

⑦ 26
+ 46

⑧ 73
+ 51

⑨ 40
+ 54

⑩ 28
+ 16

⑪ 94
+ 62

⑫ 57
+ 57

⑬ Caden played a video game for 28 minutes in the morning and 23 minutes in the afternoon. What's the total amount of time that he played?

⑭ Caden's avatar collected 76 rubies in the morning and 49 in the afternoon. How many rubies is that?

⑮ He earned 15 bonus points in the morning and 35 bonus points in the afternoon. How many bonus points did he receive for the day?

Name:_____ Date:_____

Score:
/15

① 64
+ 32

② 15
+ 95

③ 47
+ 19

④ 43
+ 67

⑤ 48
+ 47

⑥ 22
+ 18

⑦ 83
+ 78

⑧ 56
+ 27

⑨ 19
+ 12

⑩ 35
+ 66

⑪ 28
+ 54

⑫ 32
+ 87

⑬ There are 26 cars on the first train and 35 on the second train. How many cars do they have together?

⑭ The first train is carrying 89 passengers and the second train has 97. How many people are there?

⑮ Ava's family rode on the first train for 25 minutes and the second train for 15 minutes. How much time did they spend on the trains?

Name:_____ Date:_____

① 48
+ 25

② 62
+ 42

③ 61
+ 13

④ 46
+ 37

⑤ 82
+ 73

⑥ 53
+ 93

⑦ 43
+ 29

⑧ 4
+ 23

⑨ 62
+ 11

⑩ 39
+ 44

⑪ 72
+ 51

⑫ 99
+ 46

⑬ A museum has 23 stone statues and 19 bronze statues. How many statues does it have all together?

⑭ The museum had 75 ancient coins in it's collection, but will be getting 26 more. How many coins will it have then?

⑮ 42 people came to the new exhibit during the first hour and 66 people came during the second hour. How many people does that total?

Name:_____ Date:_____

① 34
+ 82

② 85
+ 37

③ 19
+ 25

④ 72
+ 18

⑤ 75
+ 45

⑥ 86
+ 64

⑦ 26
+ 41

⑧ 76
+ 27

⑨ 18
+ 94

⑩ 23
+ 84

⑪ 24
+ 14

⑫ 62
+ 67

⑬ If a mall has 36 stores on the first floor and 25 stores on the second floor, how many stores does It have?

⑭ If 82 pairs of shoes are sold one day and 93 pairs are sold the next, how many pairs are sold?

⑮ There are 56 shirts hanging on one cloths rack and 39 shirts on another. How many shirts are there?

① 98
 + 96

② 21
 + 53

③ 74
 + 8

④ 24
 + 16

⑤ 65
 + 83

⑥ 58
 + 23

⑦ 46
 + 17

⑧ 90
 + 37

⑨ 2
 + 39

⑩ 12
 + 78

⑪ 62
 + 51

⑫ 27
 + 27

⑬ An archeologist removed 48 buckets of dirt from the dig site one day and 64 buckets of dirt the next day. How many buckets of dirt were removed all together?

⑭ The archeologist found 12 bones in one location and 39 bones in another location. How many bones were found?

⑮ The archeologist spent 36 minutes cleaning one of the bones and 17 minutes cleaning another bone. What is the total amount of time it took to clean these two bones?

Name:_____ Date:_____

① 146
+ 724

② 973
+ 652

③ 215
+ 479

④ 58
+ 853

⑤ 482
+ 967

⑥ 533
+ 88

⑦ 619
+ 552

⑧ 487
+ 393

⑨ 542
+ 736

⑩ 864
+ 774

⑪ 210
+ 209

⑫ 183
+ 325

⑬ There are 856 ants in one nest and 783 ants in a second nest. What is the total number of ants these two nests contain?

⑭ The first ant nest has 327 eggs. The second nest has 314 eggs. How many eggs are there all together?

⑮ An anteater finds these nests and eats 179 ants from the first nest and 293 ants from the second nest. How many ants did the anteater eat all together?

Name:_____ Date:_____

Score: /15

① 537
+ 862

② 245
+ 931

③ 224
+ 517

④ 723
+ 83

⑤ 102
+ 163

⑥ 672
+ 953

⑦ 411
+ 349

⑧ 362
+ 895

⑨ 48
+ 383

⑩ 365
+ 491

⑪ 187
+ 63

⑫ 921
+ 757

⑬ A dentist pulled 974 teeth one year and 916 the next year. How many teeth did she pull during these two years?

⑭ The dentist placed 168 fillings this week and 205 fillings last week. How many fillings did she place in these two weeks?

⑮ The dentist gave away 315 blue toothbrushes and 482 red toothbrushes. How many toothbrushes did she give away?

① 378
  + 316

② 174
  + 551

③ 285
  + 671

④ 420
  + 519

⑤   65
  + 751

⑥ 498
  + 575

⑦ 270
  + 240

⑧   7
  + 397

⑨ 776
  + 152

⑩ 999
  + 584

⑪ 326
  + 638

⑫ 115
  + 846

⑬ Layla had 873 pictures on her computer, then she uploaded 461 more. How many are there now?

⑭ Layla's pictures were using 525 megabytes of space before she uploaded the new photos. The new photos used 194 megabytes of additional space. How many megabytes do these photos use all together?

⑮ Layla posted her favorite photos online. The first day the photos received 61 Likes. The next day they had 157 more Likes. How many Likes do they have now?

① 282
+ 134

② 670
+ 945

③ 243
+ 741

④ 662
+ 513

⑤ 523
+ 169

⑥ 408
+ 952

⑦ 94
+ 113

⑧ 816
+ 849

⑨ 337
+ 595

⑩ 618
+ 663

⑪ 813
+ 278

⑫ 699
+ 347

⑬ Grace read a book that was 204 pages long and a book that was 188 pages long. How many pages did she read?

⑭ The first Harry Potter book is 309 pages long. The second book is 341 pages long. How many pages would Grace need to read in order to read these two books?

⑮ Grace read 675 pages in January and 552 pages in February. How many pages did she read in these two months?

① 700
+ 638

② 212
+ 185

③ 823
+ 569

④ 104
+ 87

⑤ 647
+ 266

⑥ 512
+ 198

⑦ 57
+ 388

⑧ 266
+ 576

⑨ 374
+ 963

⑩ 630
+ 395

⑪ 194
+ 853

⑫ 503
+ 285

⑬ The pet shop has 329 gold fish and 127 guppies. How many fish do they have all together?

⑭ The pet shop fed the lizards 85 crickets one day and 115 crickets the next day. How many crickets did the lizards eat during these two days?

⑮ 273 puppies were sold last year. This year 328 puppies were sold. How many puppies did the pet shop sell during these two years?

① 481
  + 38

② 743
  + 106

③ 328
  + 632

④ 821
  + 513

⑤ 626
  + 754

⑥ 345
  + 874

⑦ 326
  + 354

⑧ 829
  + 572

⑨ 824
  + 412

⑩ 485
  + 586

⑪ 135
  + 475

⑫ 759
  + 348

⑬ There are 387 black cows on the farm and 152 brown cows. How many cows are there all together?

⑭ There are 209 chickens in the barn. The first day they laid 166 eggs. The second day they laid 217 eggs. What is the total number of eggs they laid during these two days?

⑮ The farm received a load of 97 bales of hay in the morning and 126 bales in the afternoon. How many bales did the farm get?

Name:_____ Date:_____

① 487
+ 809

② 254
+ 163

③ 496
+ 966

④ 425
+ 678

⑤ 123
+ 432

⑥ 312
+ 576

⑦ 427
+ 238

⑧ 576
+ 897

⑨ 376
+ 283

⑩ 154
+ 486

⑪ 893
+ 408

⑫ 347
+ 597

⑬ 156 people rode the two o'clock train and 178 people rode the five o'clock train. How many riders were there?

⑭ There were 351 people at the noon choir concert and 325 people at the evening concert. How many people saw the concert?

⑮ There are 269 girls and 236 boys that attend Hope Elementary. How many students are there?

① 2,836
+   168

② 2,385
+ 1,725

③   955
+ 8,429

④ 4,876
+ 2,648

⑤ 6,913
+ 98

⑥ 8,387
+ 2,654

⑦ 49,623
+ 93,723

⑧   478
+ 53,798

⑨ The football stadium had 5,126 fans attend the first game and 6,589 fans attend the second game. How many fans attended the two games combined?

⑩ 3,276 hot dogs were sold at the first game and 3,953 hot dogs were sold at the second game. How many hot dogs were sold all together?

Name:_____ Date:_____

Score: /10

① 5,353
+ 2,849

② 2,626
+ 4,756

③ 3,685
+ 7,146

④ 6,372
+ 3,190

⑤ 934
+ 5,368

⑥ 8,625
+ 7,154

⑦ 64,289
+ 32,743

⑧ 45,342
+ 3,458

⑨ Larry is going to build a house and shed. The house will require 4,772 bricks and the shed will need 785 bricks. How many bricks will he have to buy?

⑩ Larry is going to need 2,542 nails to build the house and 463 nails to build the shed. How many nails is that?

① 6,371
+ 8,574

② 3,689
+ 4,462

③ 7,631
+ 574

④ 2,538
+ 1,084

⑤ 6,575
+ 428

⑥ 5,832
+ 2,398

⑦ 17,593
+ 14,325

⑧ 36,798
+ 5,184

⑨ A bat leaves its cave to feed and eats 5,378 insects the first night and 6,530 insects the second night. How many insects did it eat all together?

⑩ There are 3,592 bats living in the eastern cave and 14,663 bats living in the western cave. How many bats are there in both caves combined?

Name:_____ Date:_____

① 6,563
+ 3,171

②   687
+ 2,242

③ 9,765
+ 7,394

④ 4,654
+ 5,189

⑤ 8,345
+   76

⑥ 5,983
+ 1,528

⑦ 25,725
+ 37,824

⑧ 74,238
+ 48,832

⑨ A library has 56,724 books, then it buys 3,520 more. How many books does it have now?

⑩ The library had 9,853 members last year. This year, 418 more members joined. How many members are there now?

① 9,836
+ 9,468

② 5,963
+ 3,295

③ 4,265
+ 7,624

④ 1,637
+ 2,521

⑤ 3,797
+ 1,584

⑥ 5,265
+ 6,897

⑦ 43,238
+ 47,385

⑧ 24,676
+ 63,347

⑨ An electronic store sold 792 4th generation phones and 1,582 5th generation phones. How many phones did it sell?

⑩ 416 of the 4th generation customers also bought insurance plans for their phones and 1,145 of the 5th generation customers did. How many insurance plans did the store sell?

Name:_____ Date:_____

① 521
+ 4,672

② 8,527
+ 7,529

③ 1,324
+ 3,286

④ 4,468
+ 2,483

⑤ 6,264
+ 8,852

⑥ 4,413
+ 546

⑦ 38,185
+ 85,247

⑧ 28,394
+ 14,745

⑨ A city's tallest skyscraper has 2,263 people inside of it. The second tallest skyscraper has 1,741 people inside. How many people are in these buildings combined?

⑩ A parade is taking place on main street. 8,420 people gathered on the north side of the street to watch. 7,375 people have gathered on the south side. How many people have come to watch the parade?

① 3,453
+ 5,342

② 4,483
+ 7,431

③ 2,946
+ 2,171

④ 8,295
+   267

⑤ 5,379
+ 1,485

⑥ 6,725
+ 6,815

⑦ 5,784
+ 76,147

⑧ 84,295
+ 37,941

⑨ A king spent 24,592 gold coins to have a new castle built for his royal family and spent 8,442 gold coins on decorations after it was finished. How many coins did the king spend?

⑩ The king held two feasts to celebrate the completion of the new castle. 2,183 people showed up to the first feast. 1,635 showed up to the second feast. How many people attended the two feasts combined?

Name:_____ Date:_____

①   4,538
    + 2,853

②   6,261
    + 1,358

③   2,699
    + 2,296

④   7,215
    + 9,814

⑤   853
    + 3,648

⑥   5,428
    + 2,665

⑦   57,295
    + 25,253

⑧   42,354
    + 11,745

⑨ The winter light festival used 36,391 light bulbs in it's display last year. This year it added another 4,104 light bulbs to the display. How many light bulbs are in the display now?

⑩ 25,520 people came to see the display the first week it opened, and 28,189 people came the second week. How many people came all together?

Name:_____ Date:_____

① 3,348
+ 363

② 9,744
+ 2,851

③ 3,186
+ 4,894

④ 8,142
+ 5,864

⑤ 6,865
+ 6,945

⑥ 1,317
+ 1,243

⑦ 26,973
+ 28,921

⑧ 53,483
+ 36,342

⑨ Will uses a smart watch to count how many steps he takes each day. On Monday he took 11,532 steps. On Tuesday he took 12,932. What's the total number of steps he took?

⑩ At the end of the week, Will has taken 85,322 steps. His friend Evelyn also recorded her steps. She had 91,681 steps. How many steps did the two friends take all together?

Name:_____ Date:_____

Score: /10

① 5,432
+ 3,256

② 7,968
+ 1,543

③ 9,524
+ 5,643

④ 2,386
+ 2,291

⑤ 5,832
+ 6,985

⑥ 1,325
+ 4,639

⑦ 93,623
+ 83,357

⑧ 73,669
+ 25,468

⑨ A hot dog stand ran out of hot dogs yesterday. The owner doesn't want to run out again. He plans to make 600 more hot dogs today than yesterday. If he made 3,800 hot dogs yesterday, how many will he make today?

⑩ The hot dog stand sold 2,532 bottles of soda yesterday. Today it sells 2,448 bottles. How many did it sell all together?

Name:_____ Date:_____

Score:
/10

① 7,761
+ 8,732

② 2,268
+ 4,198

③ 5,765
+ 5,167

④ 723
+ 6,581

⑤ 6,913
+ 3,576

⑥ 3,985
+ 1,376

⑦ 65,480
+ 21,574

⑧ 14,312
+ 18,866

⑨ A city is experiencing a large storm. At first 3,923 homes are without electricity, then another 1,538 homes lose power. How many homes do not have electricity now?

⑩ The next day, technicians return power to 823 homes. The day after that, 1,339 more homes regain power. How many homes have regained power during these two days?

①
```
   24
   82
+ 52
```

②
```
   15
   62
+ 85
```

③
```
    7
   91
+  9
```

④
```
   23
   65
+ 79
```

⑤
```
   25
   48
   69
+ 24
```

⑥
```
   24
   11
    3
+ 67
```

⑦
```
   90
   57
   21
+ 35
```

⑧
```
   47
   89
   41
+ 27
```

⑨ Ella, Aria, and Dan are fishing. Ella catches 26 fish. Aria catches 13, and Dan catches 15 fish. How many did they catch all together?

⑩ While fishing, they share a bag of crackers. Ella eats 17 of the crackers. Aria eats 23 crackers, and Dan eats 28 crackers. How many crackers did they eat all together?

① 32
   66
\+ 53

② 70
    5
\+ 41

③   4
    8
\+ 6

④ 25
  99
\+ 56

⑤ 10
  70
  60
\+ 30

⑥ 52
  61
  22
\+ 17

⑦ 58
  48
  36
\+ 74

⑧   4
  14
   9
\+ 26

⑨ A pet shop has 68 gold fish, 35 silver fish, and 46 black fish. How many fish does the pet shop have?

⑩ The pet shop has 23 snakes, 15 turtles, and 49 lizards. How many reptiles does the pet shop have?

Name:_____ Date:_____

① 93
95
+ 92

② 36
18
+ 15

③ 54
67
+ 43

④ 13
89
+ 47

⑤ 57
8
4
+ 55

⑥ 64
12
35
+ 26

⑦ 38
92
86
+ 70

⑧ 24
48
36
+ 54

⑨ West Elementary has 84 first graders, 78 second graders, 93 third graders, and 79 fourth graders. How many students do these grades have combined?

⑩ Some students go on a field trip to the zoo. They take three buses. The first bus has 42 students on it, the second bus has 37 students. The third bus has 40 students. How many students are going to the zoo?

Name:_____ Date:_____

① 31
　32
+ 27

② 58
　97
+ 99

③ 21
　57
+ 60

④ 66
　 7
+ 19

⑤ 75
　45
　30
+ 55

⑥ 94
　79
　86
+ 98

⑦ 24
　12
　10
+ 15

⑧ 42
　28
　16
+ 41

⑨ Riley read 38 pages in her book on Monday, 53 pages on Tuesday, 11 pages on Wednesday, and 25 pages on Thursday. How many pages did Riley read all together?

⑩ Riley gets 3 new books from the library. The first has 68 pages, the second has 98 pages, and the third has 82 pages. How many pages do these books have combined?

Name:_____ Date:_____

① 47
    31
 + 95

② 69
    26
 + 27

③ 57
    96
 + 82

④ 74
    41
 + 52

⑤   8
     7
     9
  + 5

⑥ 36
    86
     6
 + 70

⑦   7
    51
    13
  + 3

⑧ 23
     8
    74
 + 97

⑨ A farmer has 27 cows, 62 sheep and 19 pigs. How many animals does the farmer have all together?

⑩ The same farmer decides to buy 12 horses. How many animals does the farmer have after this purchase?

① 73
25
+ 65

② 24
92
+ 53

③ 35
31
+ 74

④ 49
96
+ 86

⑤ 64
24
13
+ 75

⑥ 84
97
87
+ 76

⑦ 24
3
19
+ 24

⑧ 46
78
54
+ 12

⑨ A bakery has 74 doughnuts, 91 muffins, and 68 cookies. How many items is this all together?

⑩ The bakery sells 77 muffins on Monday, 86 muffins on Tuesday, 59 muffins on Wednesday, and 94 muffins on Thursday. What is the total number of muffins the bakery sold during these four days?

Name:_____ Date:_____

Score:
/10

①
```
   45
   83
+ 23
```

②
```
   76
   42
+ 12
```

③
```
   68
   99
+ 13
```

④
```
   62
   28
+ 39
```

⑤
```
   41
   64
   21
+ 73
```

⑥
```
   84
   32
   85
+ 45
```

⑦
```
   10
   50
   95
+ 65
```

⑧
```
   33
   65
   23
+ 16
```

⑨ Isaac, Skylar, and Bella are on the same basketball team. Isaac scores 7 points, Skylar scores 12 points, and Bella scores 8 points. How many points did the three children score together?

⑩ Their team has played 4 games so far this year. They scored 45 points the first game, 36 points the second game, 31 points the third game, and 43 points the fourth game. How many points has their team scored this year?

Name:_____ Date:_____

Score: /10

①
```
   58
   64
 + 92
```

②
```
   14
   57
 + 45
```

③
```
   24
    6
 +  6
```

④
```
   74
   42
 + 11
```

⑤
```
   63
    8
    5
 + 37
```

⑥
```
   37
   95
   17
 +  4
```

⑦
```
   36
   20
   76
 + 24
```

⑧
```
   47
   24
   15
 + 59
```

⑨ Connor was at the beach and found 8 pink shells, 13 black shells, 24 white shells, and 11 grey shells. How many shells did he find all together?

⑩ Connor's mom wouldn't let him keep that many shells, so he threw 3 pink shells, 5 black shells, 16 white shells, and 6 grey shells back into the ocean. How many shells did he throw back?

① 81
37
+ 44

② 63
67
+ 63

③ 52
22
+ 18

④ 11
7
+ 14

⑤ 94
16
34
+ 72

⑥ 82
41
58
+ 67

⑦ 25
85
75
+ 30

⑧ 73
6
2
+ 56

⑨ Naomi's school is having a fundraiser. She sells 15 magazines, 38 candy bars, and 43 cookies. How many items did she sell all together?

⑩ Hudson sold 9 magazines, 27 candy bars, and 67 cookies. How many items did he sell?

① 58
14
+ 74

② 46
17
+ 9

③ 15
15
+ 60

④ 25
78
+ 41

⑤ 6
55
7
+ 83

⑥ 38
12
17
+ 26

⑦ 62
91
63
+ 83

⑧ 35
28
72
+ 46

⑨ There are three squirrels. The first hides 89 nuts, the second hides 74 nuts, and the third hides 92 nuts. How many nuts did the three squirrels hide?

⑩ the first squirrel only ate 75 of the nuts that winter. The second squirrel ate 74, and the third squirrel ate 78 nuts. How many nuts did the three squirrels eat?

Name:_____ Date:_____

Score:
/15

① 52
− 21

② 77
− 63

③ 21
− 20

④ 95
− 65

⑤ 58
− 17

⑥ 79
− 4

⑦ 58
− 26

⑧ 24
− 13

⑨ 86
− 36

⑩ 67
− 61

⑪ 45
− 2

⑫ 99
− 54

⑬ Easton had 27 pieces of candy. He ate 5 of them. How many are left?

⑭ Grandma Johnson had a bag with 58 pieces of candy in it. She gave 33 pieces away. How many are left?

⑮ Allison has 49 pieces of candy. She likes all the flavors, except blue. If she has 7 blue pieces, how many pieces have flavors that Allison likes?

Name:_____ Date:_____

① 63
− 23

② 84
− 40

③ 25
− 11

④ 58
− 31

⑤ 60
− 50

⑥ 79
− 33

⑦ 53
− 2

⑧ 42
− 22

⑨ 88
− 61

⑩ 96
− 25

⑪ 36
− 14

⑫ 84
− 73

⑬ Farmer Cora had 94 eggs but sold 54 of them. How many eggs does she have left?

⑭ Cora had 46 chickens but a fox keeps stealing them at night. If the fox has stolen 13 chickens, how many does Cora have left?

⑮ Cora's neighbor has 77 chickens. Cora buys 15 from him to replenish her flock. How many chickens does her neighbor have left?

Name:_____ Date:_____

Score:
/15

① 83
− 31

② 78
− 73

③ 95
− 40

④ 23
− 22

⑤ 87
− 57

⑥ 73
− 51

⑦ 68
− 37

⑧ 89
− 27

⑨ 55
− 4

⑩ 35
− 35

⑪ 75
− 43

⑫ 28
− 15

⑬ There are 24 stops on the bus route. The bus already stopped at 13 of them. How many stops are left?

⑭ There were 33 people on the bus, but 12 got off. How many people are left on the bus?

⑮ Jace had 25 punches on his bus pass but has used 21 of them. How many punches does he have left?

Name:_____ Date:_____

① 78
− 63

② 35
− 24

③ 23
− 11

④ 96
− 41

⑤ 48
− 13

⑥ 57
− 7

⑦ 66
− 15

⑧ 42
− 10

⑨ 84
− 3

⑩ 65
− 22

⑪ 93
− 51

⑫ 79
− 37

⑬ A hospital has 85 beds. 62 beds are currently being used. How many are not being used?

⑭ Kevin is bringing meals to all the patients. So far, he's delivered 30 meals. If there are 62 patients in the hospital, how many more meals will he have to deliver?

⑮ Sophie's doctor told her she'd have to stay in the hospital for 65 days. She's already been there 44 days. How many more days does she have to stay in the hospital?

① 73
  – 32

② 83
  – 45

③ 74
  – 23

④ 55
  – 21

⑤ 65
  – 23

⑥ 87
  – 83

⑦ 34
  – 27

⑧ 92
  – 53

⑨ 66
  – 35

⑩ 24
  – 4

⑪ 83
  – 35

⑫ 53
  – 27

⑬ There were 55 birds sitting in a tree, then 27 flew away. How many birds are left in the tree?

⑭ The birds laid a total of 90 eggs. 32 of the eggs have hatched. How many eggs have not hatched?

⑮ A total of 83 chicks were born. 45 have already learned to fly. How many have not learned to fly?

Name:_____ Date:_____

Score:

/15

① 78
− 53

② 46
− 27

③ 98
− 49

④ 35
− 17

⑤ 66
− 48

⑥ 71
− 42

⑦ 83
− 16

⑧ 75
− 13

⑨ 67
− 8

⑩ 85
− 67

⑪ 94
− 39

⑫ 43
− 28

⑬ There were 62 necklaces in a jewelry store, then a thief broke in. After the thief left, there were only 7. How many necklaces did the thief take?

⑭ There were 97 rings in the store. After the theft, there were only 23. How many rings did the thief take?

⑮ Of the 97 rings, 78 of them were diamond rings. How many of the rings did not have diamonds?

Name:_____ Date:_____

① 58
− 21

② 47
− 28

③ 83
− 17

④ 41
− 9

⑤ 53
− 46

⑥ 72
− 8

⑦ 85
− 45

⑧ 68
− 29

⑨ 74
− 19

⑩ 55
− 36

⑪ 92
− 35

⑫ 81
− 27

⑬ Faith invited 40 people to her party. 11 of the people were not able to come. How many people did come?

⑭ There were 96 slices of pizza at the party. 79 of them were eaten. How many slices of pizza are left?

⑮ There were 52 cans of soda at the party. People drank 36 of the cans. How many cans are left?

Name:_____ Date:_____

Score: /15

① 91
− 24

② 22
− 8

③ 64
− 37

④ 56
− 28

⑤ 47
− 35

⑥ 39
− 23

⑦ 81
− 13

⑧ 43
− 11

⑨ 73
− 48

⑩ 60
− 36

⑪ 32
− 16

⑫ 90
− 28

⑬ There were 76 trees in the park, but a storm blew 13 of them over. How many trees are left standing?

⑭ Of the 76 trees in the park 29 of them were oak trees. How many trees were not oak trees?

⑮ 7 of the 29 oaks trees were among the trees that fell in the storm. How many oak trees are left standing?

Name:_____ Date:_____

Score:
/15

① 55
− 17

② 64
− 59

③ 85
− 6

④ 72
− 41

⑤ 81
− 58

⑥ 21
− 5

⑦ 73
− 29

⑧ 37
− 12

⑨ 38
− 29

⑩ 92
− 26

⑪ 80
− 13

⑫ 52
− 15

⑬ There are two flocks of ducks. The first flock has 63 ducks in it. The second flock has 45 ducks. How many more ducks does the larger flock have?

⑭ The flock with 63 ducks splits apart. 28 stop to rest. The others keep flying. How many continued to fly?

⑮ How much larger is the flock of 45 ducks than this new flock of 28 ducks?

Name:_____ Date:_____

①   63
  − 17

②   45
  − 38

③   79
  − 54

④   80
  − 26

⑤   48
  − 29

⑥   94
  − 57

⑦   38
  − 15

⑧   85
  − 7

⑨   51
  − 5

⑩   60
  − 11

⑪   91
  − 43

⑫   72
  − 39

⑬ George had 60 tickets for the rides at the fair. He used 34 of the tickets. How many tickets does he have left?

⑭ Annabel has 22 tickets but wants to go on a ride that will cost 8 tickets. If she goes on this ride, how many tickets will she have left?

⑮ Ashton has 35 tickets, but his mom says he needs to give 17 of the tickets to his sister. Once he gives the tickets to her, how many tickets will Ashton have left?

Name:_____ Date:_____

Score:
/15

① 48
  − 31

② 70
  − 52

③ 57
  − 28

④ 30
  − 6

⑤ 81
  − 33

⑥ 55
  − 9

⑦ 73
  − 68

⑧ 42
  − 15

⑨ 96
  − 67

⑩ 81
  − 37

⑪ 66
  − 28

⑫ 74
  − 5

⑬ Ron is jumping on a pogo stick. His record was 59 jumps in a row, but this time he gets 83 jumps in a row. How much did he beat his record by?

⑭ Ron got 83 jumps, but his friend Morgan gets 94 jumps in a row. How much did she beat him by?

⑮ Carlos was only able to get 27 jumps. How much did Ron beat Carlos by if Ron got 83 jumps?

Name:_____ Date:_____

Score:
/15

① 91
 − 23

② 63
 − 14

③ 75
 − 8

④ 50
 − 21

⑤ 88
 − 49

⑥ 92
 − 37

⑦ 94
 − 43

⑧ 40
 − 17

⑨ 60
 − 4

⑩ 26
 − 18

⑪ 74
 − 52

⑫ 61
 − 26

⑬ Blake's basketball team lost. The score was 51 points to 42 points. How much did his team lose by?

⑭ Blake scored 9 points during the game. Someone on the other team scored 15 points. How many more points did the other player score?

⑮ Blake's team scored 16 points in the first half of the game and 26 points in the second half. How many more points did they score in the second half than the first?

① 64
  − 17

② 50
  − 38

③ 73
  − 15

④ 92
  − 27

⑤ 68
  − 40

⑥ 42
  − 13

⑦ 95
  − 58

⑧ 84
  − 49

⑨ 71
  − 22

⑩ 90
  − 54

⑪ 91
  − 17

⑫ 62
  − 45

⑬ Lauren's class has a big research project. Lauren checks out 24 books for the project. Calvin checks out 16. How many more books did Lauren check out?

⑭ Lauren asks the librarian how many books she's allowed to check out. The librarian says she can check out 40 books at a time. If Lauren already has 24 books, how many more is she allowed to check out?

⑮ Two days later Lauren returns 6 of her 24 books. How many books does she still have checked out?

Name:_____ Date:_____

Score: /15

① 74
− 28

② 93
− 77

③ 41
− 8

④ 85
− 67

⑤ 70
− 23

⑥ 52
− 16

⑦ 63
− 5

⑧ 37
− 20

⑨ 96
− 48

⑩ 60
− 35

⑪ 76
− 59

⑫ 90
− 41

⑬ Isabel is 11 years old, but her great-grandmother is 97 years old. How much older is her great-grandmother?

⑭ Isabel's father is 39 years old. How much older is Isabel's father than Isabel?

⑮ If Isabel's father is 39 and her great-grandmother is 97 years old, how much younger is her father than her great-grandmother?

Name:_____ Date:_____

Score: /15

① 862
－ 537

② 931
－ 245

③ 517
－ 224

④ 723
－ 83

⑤ 163
－ 107

⑥ 903
－ 672

⑦ 411
－ 349

⑧ 895
－ 336

⑨ 383
－ 96

⑩ 491
－ 365

⑪ 187
－ 63

⑫ 921
－ 757

⑬ A hotel has 327 rooms. 258 of the rooms are being used. How many rooms are still open?

⑭ Of the 327 rooms, 194 of them have two beds. How many rooms do not have two beds?

⑮ There are a total of 308 guests staying at the hotel. 164 of them attend the hotel's breakfast. How many people did not attend the breakfast?

① 372
− 173

② 931
− 853

③ 637
− 168

④ 451
− 268

⑤ 374
− 298

⑥ 191
− 87

⑦ 537
− 37

⑧ 210
− 135

⑨ 417
− 390

⑩ 930
− 45

⑪ 507
− 353

⑫ 363
− 127

⑬ A grocery store has 563 pineapples. It sells 516 of them. How many pineapples are left?

⑭ Last week 826 people bought coffee while shopping at the store. This week only 645 people bought coffee. How many fewer coffees were purchased?

⑮ Last week the store sold 185 bags of grapes. This week they are having a sale on grapes, and 958 bags are sold. How many more bags were sold during the sale?

① 721
– 346

② 253
– 99

③ 840
– 381

④ 600
– 142

⑤ 745
– 587

⑥ 300
– 8

⑦ 968
– 274

⑧ 463
– 414

⑨ 493
– 286

⑩ 512
– 72

⑪ 102
– 67

⑫ 643
– 189

⑬ A train has a total of 452 seats. 407 of the seats are taken. How many seats are still open?

⑭ The car attendants ask the 407 passengers if they'd like to purchase snacks during the ride. If 73 of the passengers did buy snacks, how many did not?

⑮ The train with 407 passengers makes 3 stops. Afterwards, there are only 329 passengers. How many people left the train during these stops?

Name:_____ Date:_____

Score: /15

① 785
− 653

② 846
− 557

③ 323
− 36

④ 341
− 265

⑤ 403
− 9

⑥ 682
− 548

⑦ 788
− 196

⑧ 430
− 375

⑨ 500
− 421

⑩ 346
− 312

⑪ 632
− 484

⑫ 914
− 364

⑬ There are 231 zebras in a herd. 65 of them are foals. How many zebras are not foals?

⑭ The herd of 231 zebras gets attacked by lions. None of the herd members are killed but they become so scared they split into two separate herds. If one of the herds has 149 zebras in it, how many are in the other herd?

⑮ The herd of 149 zebra's crosses a river. Only 137 of them make it past the hungry crocodiles. How many did not?

① 824
− 544

② 839
− 198

③ 714
− 89

④ 163
− 125

⑤ 300
− 242

⑥ 472
− 287

⑦ 932
− 546

⑧ 239
− 126

⑨ 513
− 478

⑩ 600
− 47

⑪ 449
− 357

⑫ 675
− 350

⑬ There were 238 carrots in Molly's garden, but rabbits ate 86 of them. How many carrots are left?

⑭ Molly harvested 422 tomatoes. She gave 374 of them to her friends. How many tomatoes are left?

⑮ Molly grew 422 tomatoes, but only 335 peppers. How many more tomatoes were there than peppers?

① 732
− 55

② 571
− 264

③ 863
− 597

④ 482
− 143

⑤ 937
− 66

⑥ 708
− 467

⑦ 395
− 284

⑧ 620
− 243

⑨ 765
− 352

⑩ 264
− 237

⑪ 617
− 388

⑫ 598
− 360

⑬ There are 945 passengers on a tropical cruise ship. 289 of them get sun burned. How many do not get sun burned?

⑭ There are 1100 life jackets on the ship. If the ship only has 945 passengers, how many extra life jackets are there?

⑮ 361 of the 945 passengers have been on a cruise ship before. How many first-time passengers are there?

Name:_____ Date:_____

① 608
－ 246

② 569
－ 173

③ 400
－ 257

④ 852
－ 625

⑤ 554
－ 9

⑥ 450
－ 275

⑦ 943
－ 856

⑧ 513
－ 70

⑨ 361
－ 191

⑩ 524
－ 179

⑪ 630
－ 12

⑫ 824
－ 726

⑬ A town is shaken by an earthquake. 429 of the town's 874 buildings are damaged. How many buildings are not damaged?

⑭ Of the 874 buildings, 874 of them have lost their electricity. How many buildings still have electricity?

⑮ Only 358 of the 874 buildings were designed to withstand an earthquake. How many were not?

① 831
− 652

② 614
− 553

③ 542
− 198

④ 102
− 66

⑤ 389
− 92

⑥ 754
− 634

⑦ 823
− 276

⑧ 673
− 345

⑨ 900
− 337

⑩ 721
− 470

⑪ 525
− 116

⑫ 632
− 483

⑬ A hospital delivered 714 babies last year and 667 babies this year. How many fewer babies were born this year?

⑭ Of the 667 babies, 328 of them were boys. How many of the babies were girls?

⑮ 16 of the 667 babies were twins. How many babies were not twins?

① 923
  − 551

② 724
  − 488

③ 200
  − 162

④ 422
  − 268

⑤ 826
  − 573

⑥ 624
  − 275

⑦ 483
  − 426

⑧ 205
  − 136

⑨ 841
  − 257

⑩ 627
  − 109

⑪ 540
  − 278

⑫ 612
  − 531

⑬ A ship carried 934 gold coins. When pirates attacked, the captain hid the coins, but 729 were found and stolen. How many coins were not stolen?

⑭ The pirates took the 729 coins and buried 250 of them. How many coins are not buried?

⑮ The pirates quickly spent the coins they didn't bury, so they returned to unbury the 250 coins. They spent 174 of those coins before deciding it'd be better to put the remaining coins in a bank. How many coins did they have left for the bank?

① 570
− 185

② 648
− 370

③ 700
− 147

④ 412
− 129

⑤ 841
− 536

⑥ 294
− 198

⑦ 375
− 207

⑧ 226
− 152

⑨ 703
− 267

⑩ 935
− 294

⑪ 501
− 72

⑫ 480
− 163

⑬ Eric and Andrea are competing in a video game. Eric scores 458 points and Andrea scores 645 points. How many more points did Andrea score?

⑭ Andrea's score of 645 points earns her a spot on the high score list. The highest score is 811 points. How many more points would she need to tie the high score?

⑮ How many more points would Eric have to add to his score of 458 in order to tie the high score of 811?

① 7,548
− 5,149

② 3,857
− 1,377

③ 6,581
− 2,586

④ 8,000
− 3,214

⑤ 6,045
− 3,891

⑥ 1,172
− 446

⑦ 63,307
− 15,753

⑧ 42,732
− 36,179

⑨ There were 6,514 files on Brad's computer. He deletes 821 of them to free up space. How many files are left?

⑩ Of the 6,514 files, 3,648 of them were photographs. How many of the files were not photographs?

© Libro Studio LLC 2019

Name:_____ Date:_____

① 8,005
− 2,216

② 7,438
− 7,167

③ 2,571
− 1,622

④ 5,100
− 3,671

⑤ 3,582
− 2,784

⑥ 6,270
− 1,266

⑦ 98,583
− 12,679

⑧ 45,732
− 18,593

⑨ 97,321 people attend the World Cup. Surveys find that 48,613 of these people want Brazil to win the match. How many of these people do not want Brazil to win?

⑩ 97,321 people attended the World Cup, but 98,000 tickets had been sold. How many tickets did not get used?

Name:_____ Date:_____

①   1,825
    − 1,139

②   7,324
    − 5,571

③   4,306
    − 1,548

④   5,000
    − 2,162

⑤   9,681
    − 5,813

⑥   3,732
    −   658

⑦   30,517
    − 18,476

⑧   52,238
    − 47,903

⑨ Archeologists found two mummies. The first is believed to be 5,380 years old. The second is thought to be 3,612 years old. How much older is the first?

⑩ 1,547 hieroglyphic images were carved inside the first tomb. 2,142 hieroglyphic images were carved inside the second tomb. How many more images were inside the second tomb?

① 4,000
– 1,592

② 5,819
– 3,506

③ 8,712
– 2,835

④ 7,621
– 5,059

⑤ 6,072
– 3,829

⑥ 3,681
– 3,528

⑦ 60,000
– 21,073

⑧ 11,735
– 7,827

⑨ A paper factory makes 83,067 white sheets of paper and 15,063 blue sheets of paper each month. How many more white sheets does it produce each month?

⑩ A machine in the factory breaks down. It takes a couple days to fix it. The factory owner estimates that 8,423 fewer white sheets will be printed this month because of the issue. If the owner had originally expected to produce 83,067 white sheets this month, how many white sheets do they expect to print now?

Name:_____ Date:_____

① 9,493
− 1,675

② 5,718
− 2,993

③ 7,401
− 3,383

④ 8,148
− 1,761

⑤ 3,050
−   83

⑥ 4,731
− 3,651

⑦ 50,470
− 26,521

⑧ 84,834
− 42,385

⑨ 4,235 fireworks are launched for a celebration. 385 of them are duds and don't explode like they're supposed to. How many fireworks do explode?

⑩ The fireworks are launched over a river. 36,750 people gather on the east side to watch the show. 45,862 people gather on the west side. How many more people gathered on the west side?

Name:_____ Date:_____

Score:
/10

① 4,005
− 1,162

② 9,074
− 3,175

③ 7,863
− 7,294

④ 3,185
− 2,469

⑤ 5,583
− 2,648

⑥ 4,592
− 3,551

⑦ 74,836
− 56,578

⑧ 26,478
− 8,380

⑨ Ariel is trying to put together a 10,000-piece puzzle. She has 3,472 of the pieces together already. How many more pieces does she have left?

⑩ Ariel steps away from her 10,000-piece puzzle and takes a bathroom break. When she returns, she finds that her little brother took 361 puzzle pieces from the table. How many of the pieces are still on the table?

Name:_____ Date:_____

① 7,563
 − 3,171

② 5,200
 − 3,473

③ 4,845
 − 1,758

④ 6,000
 −   174

⑤ 9,368
 − 6,731

⑥ 3,580
 − 2,687

⑦ 63,845
 − 30,199

⑧ 96,150
 − 18,734

⑨ A photographer goes to many schools and takes 5,732 pictures of students. 3 weeks later he returns for 1,575 retakes. How many more pictures were taken on the original picture day?

⑩ 4,047 of the students order their school photo. 1,862 of them pay more for the deluxe package. How many of these students did not order the deluxe package?

Name:_____ Date:_____

Score: /10

① 6,482
− 2,068

② 4,868
− 3,990

③ 7,165
− 2,385

④ 1,001
− 746

⑤ 9,053
− 6,821

⑥ 3,206
− 2,528

⑦ 81,517
− 26,618

⑧ 36,035
− 25,518

⑨ 23,104 people come to see a new movie at the theater. The theater had only expected about 16,500 people to watch it. How many more showed up than expected?

⑩ Of these 23,104 people, 18,351 ordered popcorn. How many did not order popcorn?

Name:_____ Date:_____

① 3,733
− 3,251

② 5,826
− 1,092

③ 5,000
− 2,394

④ 4,162
− 3,683

⑤ 7,345
− 4,713

⑥ 5,983
− 1,528

⑦ 35,725
− 27,824

⑧ 74,238
− 48,832

⑨ Julia had 2,084 unread emails when she returned from vacation. Luckily, most of them went straight to her spam folder. 326 emails did not. How many emails went straight to her spam folder?

⑩ Julia started reading the 326 emails. She decided to take a break after reading 137 of them. How many more emails does she have left to read?

Name:_____ Date:_____

Score: /10

① 6,563
 − 3,171

② 6,242
 − 2,287

③ 9,765
 − 7,394

④ 5,189
 − 4,616

⑤ 8,345
 −   76

⑥ 5,983
 − 1,528

⑦ 63,265
 − 25,834

⑧ 92,040
 − 35,752

⑨ A football stadium had 5,126 people attend the first game and 6,589 people attend the second game. How many more people attended the second game?

⑩ 3,276 hot dogs were sold at the first game and 3,953 hot dogs were sold at the second game. How many more hot dogs were sold at the second game?

Name:_____ Date:_____

① 72
　+ 43

② 87
　− 28

③ 415
　− 237

④ 382
　+ 493

⑤ 128
　+ 64

⑥ 43
　− 17

⑦ 626
　+ 284

⑧ 700
　− 514

⑨ 502
　− 86

⑩ 29
　+ 97

⑪ 328
　+ 460

⑫ 861
　− 835

⑬ Two scuba divers go for a swim. Kyle dives 34 meters below the surface. Alex dives 25 meters down. How much deeper did Kyle swim?

⑭ They count the number of sharks they see. Kyle sees 54 and Alex sees 68. How many sharks do they see combined?

⑮ Their tanks each had 120 minutes of air when they began their dive. When they finished, there was only 32 minutes left. How long was their dive?

Name:_____ Date:_____

① 122
– 67

② 453
– 258

③ 739
+ 94

④ 51
– 14

⑤ 69
+ 553

⑥ 64
+ 78

⑦ 600
– 136

⑧ 523
+ 974

⑨ 472
– 412

⑩ 706
– 247

⑪ 198
+ 352

⑫ 83
+ 49

⑬ The mountain had 473 skiers and 154 snowboarders. How many people were there all together?

⑭ How many more skiers were there than snowboarders?

⑮ At the lodge, 329 people had hot chocolate and 168 had coffee. How many more hot chocolate drinkers were there?

Name:_____ Date:_____

① 72
  − 24

② 82
  + 67

③ 591
  − 413

④ 739
  + 842

⑤ 147
  + 385

⑥ 724
  − 263

⑦ 308
  − 162

⑧ 557
  + 84

⑨ 25
  + 190

⑩ 400
  − 361

⑪ 503
  + 342

⑫ 70
  + 6

⑬ Payton and Aubree are making necklaces. Payton's had 143 beads on it. Aubree had 182 beads on hers. How many beads have they used all together?

⑭ How many more beads does Aubree's necklace have than Payton's?

⑮ Payton decides to add another 78 beads to her 143-bead necklace. How many beads does her necklace have now?

© Libro Studio LLC 2019

Name:_____ Date:_____

Score: /15

① 459
+ 736

② 570
− 84

③ 652
+ 73

④ 334
− 317

⑤ 603
− 368

⑥ 482
+ 184

⑦ 946
+ 989

⑧ 63
− 39

⑨ 44
+ 478

⑩ 151
− 76

⑪ 721
− 694

⑫ 480
+ 731

⑬ The pet shop had 738 gold fish and 365 silver fish. How many fish is that together?

⑭ How many more goldfish are there than silver fish?

⑮ The pet shop sells 253 of the 738 gold fish. How many gold fish are left?

① 746
− 184

② 953
+ 682

③ 275
+ 479

④   58
+ 463

⑤ 582
+ 957

⑥ 533
− 88

⑦ 619
− 552

⑧ 887
+ 363

⑨ 342
+ 773

⑩ 864
− 774

⑪ 210
− 209

⑫ 283
+ 326

⑬ There are 158 walruses and 274 sea lions on the same beach. How many more sea lions are there than walruses?

⑭ There are 274 sea lions on the beach, until 186 of them go into the water to hunt for fish. How many are left on the beach?

⑮ There were 274 sea lions, then 53 sea lion pups were born. How many sea lions are there now?

① 837
− 562

② 245
+ 931

③ 224
+ 517

④ 723
− 83

⑤ 102
+ 163

⑥ 953
− 672

⑦ 411
− 349

⑧ 362
+ 895

⑨ 68
+ 583

⑩ 365
+ 491

⑪ 187
− 63

⑫ 921
− 757

⑬ Rachel picks 251 apples and John picks 264 apples. How many apples did they pick together?

⑭ How many more apples did John pick than Rachel?

⑮ Rachel sells 173 of her 251 apples at the farmer's market. How many apples does she have left?

Name:_____ Date:_____

① 498
  – 414

② 574
  – 158

③ 253
  + 671

④ 220
  + 517

⑤ 812
  – 62

⑥ 998
  – 575

⑦ 751
  + 420

⑧ 8
  + 595

⑨ 776
  – 152

⑩ 999
  – 584

⑪ 326
  + 638

⑫ 115
  + 846

⑬ 953 people are at the beach. 267 of them are in the water. How many are still on land?

⑭ Of the 267 people in the water, 73 of them are surfing. How many non-surfers are in the water?

⑮ An ice cream vendor is at the beach too. 198 of the 953 people at the beach buy ice cream. How many do not?

Name:_____ Date:_____

Score:
/15

① 282
− 134

② 670
+ 965

③ 275
+ 741

④ 662
− 513

⑤ 523
− 169

⑥ 509
+ 952

⑦ 94
+ 223

⑧ 827
− 348

⑨ 337
+ 595

⑩ 618
+ 663

⑪ 813
− 278

⑫ 699
− 347

⑬ Brad has 672 baseball cards in his collection. Tim has 845 baseball cards. How many cards do they have together?

⑭ How many more cards does Tim have than Brad?

⑮ Tim got some money for his birthday. He used it to buy 243 more baseball cards. How many does he have now?

Name:_____ Date:_____

Score: /15

① 700
  − 638

② 262
  + 185

③ 813
  − 569

④ 105
  − 88

⑤ 747
  + 255

⑥ 523
  + 298

⑦ 57
  + 388

⑧ 741
  − 576

⑨ 392
  + 973

⑩ 631
  − 395

⑪ 183
  + 253

⑫ 543
  − 285

⑬ Bill read 557 pages, Kaylee read 389 pages, and Josh read 626 pages. How many did Bill and Josh read together?

⑭ How many did Kaylee and Bill read together?

⑮ How many more did Josh read than Kaylee?

Name:_____ Date:_____

Score:
/15

① 485
− 58

② 754
+ 108

③ 315
+ 631

④ 821
− 513

⑤ 659
+ 254

⑥ 652
+ 974

⑦ 426
− 354

⑧ 829
− 572

⑨ 824
− 412

⑩ 485
+ 586

⑪ 135
+ 475

⑫ 759
− 348

⑬ Khloe picked 147 flowers. Melody picked 173. How many flowers did they pick together?

⑭ How many more did Melody pick than Khloe?

⑮ By the time Melody got home, 36 of her flowers had wilted. How many of her 173 flowers had not wilted?

① 463
+ 609

② 254
− 163

③ 956
− 269

④ 443
+ 678

⑤ 474
− 438

⑥ 324
+ 576

⑦ 427
− 238

⑧ 547
+ 897

⑨ 376
− 283

⑩ 713
+ 486

⑪ 893
− 408

⑫ 63
+ 597

⑬ An auto repair shop fixed 248 vehicles today. 76 were trucks. How many vehicles were not trucks?

⑭ Today they fixed 248 vehicles, but yesterday they fixed 283 vehicles. How many more vehicles did they fix yesterday?

⑮ How many vehicles did they fix both days together?

① 946
− 758

② 763
+ 572

③ 615
− 479

④   58
+ 873

⑤ 428
− 367

⑥ 633
+ 69

⑦ 319
+ 523

⑧ 741
− 193

⑨ 642
− 376

⑩ 864
+ 774

⑪ 252
+ 569

⑫ 983
− 354

⑬ A post office received 756 letters yesterday and 962 letters today. How many letters is that?

⑭ How many more letters did the post office receive today than yesterday?

⑮ Of the 756 letters received yesterday, 583 of the letters were already delivered today. How many of yesterday's letters were not delivered?

Name:_____ Date:_____

Score: /15

① 537
  − 54

② 279
  + 431

③ 824
  − 517

④ 723
  + 631

⑤ 834
  + 167

⑥ 72
  − 53

⑦ 400
  − 349

⑧ 362
  + 545

⑨ 642
  − 383

⑩ 341
  + 491

⑪ 187
  + 63

⑫ 603
  − 357

⑬ There are two old oak trees. The first is 327 years old. The second is 265 years old. How much older is the first oak tree?

⑭ How much longer will the first oak tree need to live in order to be 400 years old?

⑮ How much longer would the second oak tree need to live in order to be 400 years old?

Name:_____ Date:_____

Score: /15

① 678
+ 619

② 674
− 551

③ 285
+ 671

④ 890
− 519

⑤ 312
− 251

⑥ 98
+ 57

⑦ 789
+ 231

⑧ 624
− 266

⑨ 776
+ 955

⑩ 947
− 284

⑪ 86
−38

⑫ 471
+ 846

⑬ There were 339 vehicles stuck in a traffic jam yesterday. Today there are only 181 vehicles in a traffic jam. How many more vehicles were in yesterday's jam?

⑭ Another 97 vehicles join today's traffic jam. How many vehicles are in the traffic jam now?

⑮ Roger's family is stuck in the traffic jam. Their drive was only supposed to take 13 minutes. Now their GPS estimates that it will take them 37 minutes. How much longer is that?

Name:_____ Date:_____

① 459
+ 134

② 920
− 345

③ 243
+ 741

④ 732
− 475

⑤ 723
+ 128

⑥ 850
− 152

⑦ 94
+ 73

⑧ 816
+ 849

⑨ 84
− 19

⑩ 618
− 163

⑪ 683
+ 278

⑫ 624
+ 137

⑬ 378 bees are currently inside of a hive. Another 553 bees live in the hive but are gone to collect food. How many bees live in the hive all together?

⑭ How many more bees are gone to collect food than currently in the hive?

⑮ A bear finds the hive and wants honey. Many of the 378 bees attack the bear. 127 of them do not survive. How many of the 378 did survive?

Name:_____ Date:_____

Score: /15

① 65
+ 638

② 56
− 37

③ 823
− 285

④ 571
+ 74

⑤ 917
− 236

⑥ 126
+ 198

⑦ 657
− 372

⑧ 381
+ 576

⑨ 621
− 63

⑩ 436
+ 368

⑪ 514
− 353

⑫ 517
+ 245

⑬ Kelly wants to download 2 apps onto her phone. Together they will use 472 megabytes of space. If the first app requires 217 megabytes, how many megabytes does the second app require?

⑭ Kelly only has 431 megabytes of free space on her phone. How much more space is needed to download both apps?

⑮ Kelly only downloads the app that requires 217 megabytes of space. How much free space does her phone have after the download?

Name:_____ Date:_____

① 481
+ 283

② 543
− 176

③ 628
− 432

④ 391
+ 513

⑤ 626
− 554

⑥ 445
− 74

⑦ 615
+ 354

⑧ 245
+ 572

⑨ 61
− 12

⑩ 648
+ 373

⑪ 935
− 475

⑫ 78
+ 49

⑬ Iris scored 87 points on her first test and 99 points on her second test. How many points is this together?

⑭ How many more points did Iris earn on her second test compared to the first test?

⑮ Tyler only scored 73 points on the second test. How many more points did Iris score on the second test than Tyler?

Name:_____ Date:_____

① 487
− 209

② 744
+ 163

③ 746
+ 396

④ 915
− 578

⑤ 421
+ 432

⑥ 72
− 34

⑦ 427
+ 238

⑧ 576
+ 978

⑨ 531
− 233

⑩ 654
− 486

⑪ 800
− 612

⑫ 44
+ 97

⑬ It took Reese 55 minutes to finish her reading assignment and 32 minutes to complete her math assignment. How much time did it take her to complete these assignments?

⑭ It took Carter 53 minutes to finish the same reading assignment and 49 minutes to finish the math assignment. How long did it take him to complete these assignments?

⑮ How much longer did it take Carter to finish the math assignment than Reese?

Name:_____ Date:_____

Score:
/15

① 478
+ 566

② 264
+ 681

③ 615
– 431

④ 800
– 274

⑤ 467
– 91

⑥ 329
+ 768

⑦ 345
+ 875

⑧ 425
– 397

⑨ 456
– 152

⑩ 486
– 235

⑪ 625
+ 638

⑫ 115
+ 846

⑬ Paige has a 96-pack of colored pencils and a 120-pack of crayons. How many items is this all together?

⑭ Oscar has a 112 pack of colored pencils and a 48-pack of crayons. How many items is this all together?

⑮ How many more colored pencils does Oscar have than Paige?

Name:_____ Date:_____

Score:
/15

① 923
− 134

② 670
+ 461

③ 713
− 541

④ 623
+ 884

⑤ 653
− 186

⑥ 835
+ 765

⑦ 94
− 25

⑧ 468
+ 149

⑨ 37
+ 95

⑩ 275
+ 663

⑪ 842
− 267

⑫ 600
− 347

⑬ Gracie had 116 people come to her Piano recital last year. This year 231 people came to her recital. How many more people came this year?

⑭ The music hall can seat 300 people. If 231 people came to the recital, how many more could have fit into the music hall?

⑮ Gracie didn't expect so many people to attend the recital. She had bought 125 cookies to give the attendants but decided she should buy 125 more. How many cookies is that all together?

Name:_____ Date:_____

① 300
+ 172

② 372
− 184

③ 744
+ 569

④ 103
− 35

⑤ 647
− 487

⑥ 725
+ 396

⑦ 67
+ 278

⑧ 966
− 576

⑨ 531
− 263

⑩ 630
+ 395

⑪ 483
+ 721

⑫ 876
− 585

⑬ Jonah loves bowling. He scored 236 points during his first game and 179 points during his second game. How many points is that together?

⑭ How many more points did he score during the first game compared to the second game?

⑮ How many more points would he have needed to score during the first game in order to bowl a perfect 300-point game?

Name:_____ Date:_____

Score: /15

① 611
− 265

② 863
+ 238

③ 528
− 432

④ 654
+ 513

⑤ 765
+ 754

⑥ 42
+ 74

⑦ 726
− 376

⑧ 827
− 564

⑨ 354
− 278

⑩ 485
+ 357

⑪ 68
− 29

⑫ 546
+ 186

⑬ Brooke and Dale send out 174 invitations for their wedding. They get a response for 96 of these invitations. How many of the invitations have not received a response?

⑭ 285 people attend Brooke and Dale's wedding. They had expected 306 people to attend. How many fewer people attended than they expected?

⑮ Brooke and Dale plan to send 214 thank you cards to those that gave them gifts. So far, they have sent out 73 thank you cards. How many more cards do they plan to send?

Name:_____ Date:_____

Score:
/15

① 787
− 209

② 828
+ 473

③ 523
− 396

④ 425
+ 749

⑤ 832
− 276

⑥ 729
+ 576

⑦ 56
− 28

⑧ 64
+ 496

⑨ 86
+ 83

⑩ 854
− 476

⑪ 456
+ 786

⑫ 547
− 497

⑬ Farmer Jesse has 913 tomato plants. His neighbor Fiona only has 638 tomato plants. How many tomato plants do they have combined?

⑭ How many more tomato plants does Jesse have than Fiona?

⑮ Jesse's pigs escape from their pen. They eat and trample 464 of his tomato plants. How many tomato plants does he have left?

Name:_____ Date:_____

① 934
  + 958

② 500
  + 146

③ 57
  + 79

④ 83
  − 46

⑤ 416
  − 83

⑥ 786
  + 265

⑦ 803
  − 456

⑧ 528
  + 935

⑨ 345
  + 256

⑩ 915
  − 198

⑪ 475
  − 131

⑫ 86
  + 179

⑬ Haylee and Caleb both want to be president of the yearbook committee. A school vote is held. Haylee receives 358 votes. Caleb receives 327 votes. How many people voted?

⑭ How many more votes did Haylee receive then Caleb?

⑮ Of the 362 girls that voted, 279 voted for Haylee. How many girls voted for Caleb?

Name:_____ Date:_____

① 704
− 375

② 465
+ 145

③ 413
− 243

④ 456
+ 36

⑤ 72
+ 48

⑥ 345
− 189

⑦ 641
+ 274

⑧ 800
− 526

⑨ 874
+ 652

⑩ 630
− 152

⑪ 673
+ 853

⑫ 562
− 485

⑬ Elliot posts a video online. It receives 38 views during the first day and 426 additional views the second day. How many views is that all together?

⑭ How many more views did the video receive the second day than the first day?

⑮ On the third day, the video receives 892 additional views. How many more views did it receive the third day than the second day?

Name:_____ Date:_____

Score: /15

① 507
− 213

② 375
− 83

③ 408
+ 96

④ 427
+ 689

⑤ 962
− 184

⑥ 58
+ 47

⑦ 435
+ 175

⑧ 617
− 258

⑨ 793
+ 372

⑩ 453
− 418

⑪ 84
− 57

⑫ 428
+ 786

⑬ Racecars need to complete 500 laps to finish the Northern Cup Race. Clara's car crashes after 218 laps. How many more laps did she have left?

⑭ Jason is also competing in the Northern Cup Race. His car crashed after 376 laps. How many laps did he have left?

⑮ How many more laps did Jason's car complete than Clara's car?

Answer Key

Day 1: (1) 98 (2) 57 (3) 89 (4) 78
(5) 46 (6) 95 (7) 36 (8) 87
(9) 86 (10) 59 (11) 38 (12) 68
(13) 26 kids (14) 95 kids (15) 33 kids

Day 2: (1) 86 (2) 58 (3) 49 (4) 86
(5) 18 (6) 57 (7) 84 (8) 46
(9) 65 (10) 37 (11) 59 (12) 96
(13) 56 points (14) 19 points (15) 27 girls

Day 3: (1) 24 (2) 49 (3) 63 (4) 67
(5) 36 (6) 49 (7) 51 (8) 87
(9) 35 (10) 84 (11) 58 (12) 18
(13) 15 books (14) 55 books (15) 78 books

Day 4: (1) 35 (2) 72 (3) 37 (4) 25
(5) 59 (6) 54 (7) 79 (8) 84
(9) 48 (10) 38 (11) 76 (12) 18
(13) 94 letters (14) 86 homes (15) 27 invitations

Day 5: (1) 84 (2) 76 (3) 141 (4) 45
(5) 105 (6) 73 (7) 63 (8) 116
(9) 93 (10) 40 (11) 158 (12) 84
(13) 52 snakes (14) 45 monkeys (15) 73 penguins

Day 6: (1) 38 (2) 128 (3) 91 (4) 159
(5) 77 (6) 95 (7) 60 (8) 139
(9) 111 (10) 117 (11) 140 (12) 102
(13) 55 minutes (14) 62 fish (15) 41 worms

Day 7: (1) 51 (2) 179 (3) 77 (4) 32
(5) 112 (6) 65 (7) 114 (8) 119
(9) 84 (10) 21 (11) 122 (12) 116
(13) 41 starfish (14) 44 dolphins (15) 85 people

Day 8: (1) 185 (2) 88 (3) 44 (4) 167
(5) 150 (6) 116 (7) 72 (8) 124
(9) 94 (10) 44 (11) 156 (12) 114
(13) 51 minutes (14) 125 rubies (15) 50 bonus points

Day 9: (1) 96 (2) 110 (3) 66 (4) 110
(5) 95 (6) 40 (7) 161 (8) 83
(9) 31 (10) 101 (11) 82 (12) 119
(13) 61 cars (14) 186 people (15) 40 minutes

Day 10: (1) 73 (2) 104 (3) 74 (4) 83
(5) 155 (6) 146 (7) 72 (8) 27
(9) 73 (10) 83 (11) 123 (12) 145
(13) 42 statues (14) 101 coins (15) 108 people

Day 11: (1) 116 (2) 122 (3) 44 (4) 90
(5) 120 (6) 150 (7) 67 (8) 103
(9) 112 (10) 107 (11) 38 (12) 129
(13) 61 stores (14) 175 pairs (15) 95 shirts

Day 12: (1) 194 (2) 74 (3) 82 (4) 40
(5) 148 (6) 81 (7) 63 (8) 127
(9) 41 (10) 90 (11) 113 (12) 54
(13) 112 buckets (14) 51 bones (15) 53 minutes

Day 13: (1) 870 (2) 1,625 (3) 694 (4) 911
(5) 1,449 (6) 621 (7) 1,171 (8) 880
(9) 1,278 (10) 1,638 (11) 419 (12) 508
(13) 1,639 ants (14) 641 eggs (15) 472 ants

Day 14: (1) 1,399 (2) 1,176 (3) 741 (4) 806
(5) 265 (6) 1,625 (7) 760 (8) 1,257
(9) 431 (10) 856 (11) 250 (12) 1,678
(13) 1,890 teeth (14) 373 fillings (15) 797 toothbrushes

Day 15: (1) 694 (2) 725 (3) 956 (4) 939
(5) 816 (6) 1,073 (7) 510 (8) 404
(9) 928 (10) 1,583 (11) 964 (12) 961
(13) 1,334 pictures (14) 719 megabytes (15) 218 Likes

Day 16: (1) 416 (2) 1,615 (3) 984 (4) 1,175
(5) 692 (6) 1,360 (7) 207 (8) 1,665
(9) 932 (10) 1,281 (11) 1,091 (12) 1,046
(13) 392 pages (14) 650 pages (15) 1,227 pages

Day 17: (1) 1,338 (2) 397 (3) 1,392 (4) 191
(5) 913 (6) 710 (7) 445 (8) 842
(9) 1,337 (10) 1,025 (11) 1,047 (12) 788
(13) 456 fish (14) 200 crickets (15) 601 puppies

Day 18: (1) 519 (2) 849 (3) 960 (4) 1,334
(5) 1,380 (6) 1,219 (7) 680 (8) 1,401
(9) 1,236 (10) 1,071 (11) 610 (12) 1,107
(13) 539 cows (14) 383 eggs (15) 223 bales

Day 19: (1) 1,296 (2) 417 (3) 1,462 (4) 1,103
(5) 555 (6) 888 (7) 665 (8) 1,473
(9) 659 (10) 640 (11) 1,301 (12) 944
(13) 334 people (14) 676 people (15) 505 students

Day 20: (1) 3,004 (2) 4,110 (3) 9,384
(4) 7,524 (5) 7,011 (6) 11,041
(7) 143,346 (8) 54,276
(9) 11,715 fans (10) 7,229 hot dogs

Answer Key

Day 21: (1) 8,202   (2) 7,382   (3) 10,831   (4) 9,562   (5) 6,302   (6) 15,779   (7) 97,032   (8) 48,800   (9) 5,557 bricks   (10) 3,005 nails

Day 22: (1) 14,945   (2) 8,151   (3) 8,205   (4) 3,622   (5) 7,003   (6) 8,230   (7) 31,918   (8) 41,982   (9) 11,908 insects   (10) 18,255 bats

Day 23: (1) 9,734   (2) 2,929   (3) 17,159   (4) 9,843   (5) 8,421   (6) 7,511   (7) 63,549   (8) 123,070   (9) 60,244 books   (10) 10,271 members

Day 24: (1) 19,304   (2) 9,258   (3) 11,889   (4) 4,158   (5) 5,381   (6) 12,162   (7) 90,623   (8) 88,023   (9) 2,374 phones   (10) 1,561 insurance plans

Day 25: (1) 5,193   (2) 16,056   (3) 4,610   (4) 6,951   (5) 15,116   (6) 4,959   (7) 123,432   (8) 43,139   (9) 4,004 people   (10) 15,795 people

Day 26: (1) 8,795   (2) 11,914   (3) 5,117   (4) 8,562   (5) 6,864   (6) 13,540   (7) 81,931   (8) 122,236   (9) 33,034 coins   (10) 3,818 people

Day 27: (1) 7,391   (2) 7,619   (3) 4,995   (4) 17,029   (5) 4,501   (6) 8,093   (7) 82,548   (8) 54,099   (9) 40,495 light bulbs   (10) 53,709 people

Day 28: (1) 3,711   (2) 12,595   (3) 8,080   (4) 14,006   (5) 13,810   (6) 2,560   (7) 55,894   (8) 89,825   (9) 24,464 steps   (10) 177,003 steps

Day 29: (1) 8,688   (2) 9,511   (3) 15,167   (4) 4,677   (5) 12,817   (6) 5,964   (7) 176,980   (8) 99,137   (9) 4,400 hot dogs   (10) 4,980 bottles

Day 30: (1) 16,493   (2) 6,466   (3) 10,932   (4) 7,304   (5) 10,489   (6) 5,361   (7) 87,054   (8) 33,178   (9) 5,461 homes   (10) 2,162 homes

Day 31: (1) 158   (2) 162   (3) 107   (4) 167   (5) 166   (6) 105   (7) 203   (8) 204   (9) 54 fish   (10) 68 crackers

Day 32: (1) 151   (2) 116   (3) 18   (4) 180   (5) 170   (6) 152   (7) 216   (8) 53   (9) 149 fish   (10) 87 reptiles

Day 33: (1) 280   (2) 69   (3) 164   (4) 149   (5) 124   (6) 137   (7) 286   (8) 162   (9) 334 students   (10) 119 students

Day 34: (1) 90   (2) 254   (3) 138   (4) 92   (5) 205   (6) 357   (7) 61   (8) 127   (9) 127 pages   (10) 248 pages

Day 35: (1) 173   (2) 122   (3) 235   (4) 167   (5) 29   (6) 198   (7) 74   (8) 202   (9) 108 animals   (10) 120 animals

Day 36: (1) 163   (2) 169   (3) 140   (4) 231   (5) 176   (6) 344   (7) 70   (8) 190   (9) 233 items   (10) 316 muffins

Day 37: (1) 151   (2) 130   (3) 180   (4) 129   (5) 199   (6) 246   (7) 220   (8) 137   (9) 27 points   (10) 155 points

Day 38: (1) 214   (2) 116   (3) 36   (4) 127   (5) 113   (6) 153   (7) 156   (8) 145   (9) 56 shells   (10) 30 shells

Day 39: (1) 162   (2) 193   (3) 92   (4) 32   (5) 216   (6) 248   (7) 215   (8) 137   (9) 96 items   (10) 103 items

Day 40: (1) 146   (2) 72   (3) 90   (4) 144   (5) 151   (6) 93   (7) 299   (8) 181   (9) 255 nuts   (10) 227 nuts

Answer Key

Day 41: (1) 31   (2) 14   (3) 1   (4) 30
(5) 41   (6) 75   (7) 32   (8) 11
(9) 50   (10) 6   (11) 43   (12) 45
(13) 22 pieces (14) 25 pieces (15) 42 pieces

Day 42: (1) 40   (2) 44   (3) 14   (4) 27
(5) 10   (6) 46   (7) 51   (8) 20
(9) 27   (10) 71   (11) 22   (12) 11
(13) 40 eggs (14) 33 chickens (15) 62 chickens

Day 43: (1) 52   (2) 5   (3) 55   (4) 1
(5) 30   (6) 22   (7) 31   (8) 62
(9) 51   (10) 0   (11) 32   (12) 13
(13) 11 stops (14) 21 people (15) 4 punches

Day 44: (1) 15   (2) 11   (3) 12   (4) 55
(5) 35   (6) 50   (7) 51   (8) 32
(9) 81   (10) 43   (11) 42   (12) 42
(13) 23 beds (14) 32 meals (15) 21 days

Day 45: (1) 41   (2) 38   (3) 51   (4) 34
(5) 42   (6) 4   (7) 7   (8) 39
(9) 31   (10) 20   (11) 48   (12) 26
(13) 28 birds (14) 58 eggs (15) 38 chicks

Day 46: (1) 25   (2) 19   (3) 49   (4) 18
(5) 18   (6) 29   (7) 67   (8) 62
(9) 59   (10) 18   (11) 55   (12) 15
(13) 55 necklaces (14) 74 rings (15) 19 rings

Day 47: (1) 37   (2) 19   (3) 66   (4) 32
(5) 7   (6) 64   (7) 40   (8) 39
(9) 55   (10) 19   (11) 57   (12) 54
(13) 29 people (14) 17 slices (15) 16 cans

Day 48: (1) 67   (2) 14   (3) 27   (4) 28
(5) 12   (6) 16   (7) 68   (8) 32
(9) 25   (10) 24   (11) 16   (12) 62
(13) 63 trees (14) 47 oak trees (15) 22 oak trees

Day 49: (1) 38   (2) 5   (3) 79   (4) 31
(5) 23   (6) 16   (7) 44   (8) 25
(9) 9   (10) 66   (11) 67   (12) 37
(13) 18 ducks (14) 35 ducks (15) 17 ducks

Day 50: (1) 46   (2) 7   (3) 25   (4) 54
(5) 19   (6) 37   (7) 23   (8) 78
(9) 46   (10) 49   (11) 48   (12) 33
(13) 26 tickets (14) 14 tickets (15) 18 tickets

Day 51: (1) 17   (2) 18   (3) 29   (4) 24
(5) 48   (6) 46   (7) 5   (8) 27
(9) 29   (10) 44   (11) 38   (12) 69
(13) 24 jumps (14) 11 jumps (15) 56 jumps

Day 52: (1) 68   (2) 49   (3) 67   (4) 29
(5) 39   (6) 55   (7) 51   (8) 23
(9) 56   (10) 8   (11) 22   (12) 35
(13) 9 points (14) 6 points (15) 10 points

Day 53: (1) 47   (2) 12   (3) 58   (4) 65
(5) 28   (6) 29   (7) 37   (8) 35
(9) 49   (10) 36   (11) 74   (12) 17
(13) 8 books (14) 16 books (15) 18 books

Day 54: (1) 46   (2) 16   (3) 33   (4) 18
(5) 47   (6) 36   (7) 58   (8) 17
(9) 48   (10) 25   (11) 17   (12) 49
(13) 86 years (14) 28 years (15) 58 years

Day 55: (1) 325   (2) 686   (3) 293   (4) 640
(5) 56   (6) 231   (7) 62   (8) 559
(9) 287   (10) 126   (11) 124   (12) 164
(13) 69 rooms (14) 133 rooms (15) 144 people

Day 56: (1) 199   (2) 78   (3) 469   (4) 183
(5) 76   (6) 104   (7) 500   (8) 75
(9) 27   (10) 885   (11) 154   (12) 236
(13) 47 pineapples (14) 181 people (15) 773 bags

Day 57: (1) 375   (2) 154   (3) 459   (4) 458
(5) 158   (6) 292   (7) 694   (8) 49
(9) 207   (10) 440   (11) 35   (12) 454
(13) 45 seats (14) 334 passengers (15) 78 passengers

Day 58: (1) 132   (2) 289   (3) 287   (4) 76
(5) 394   (6) 134   (7) 592   (8) 55
(9) 79   (10) 34   (11) 148   (12) 550
(13) 166 zebras (14) 82 zebras (15) 12 zebras

Day 59: (1) 280   (2) 641   (3) 625   (4) 38
(5) 58   (6) 185   (7) 386   (8) 113
(9) 35   (10) 553   (11) 92   (12) 325
(13) 152 carrots (14) 48 tomatoes (15) 87 more tomatoes

Day 60: (1) 677   (2) 307   (3) 266   (4) 339
(5) 871   (6) 241   (7) 111   (8) 377
(9) 413   (10) 27   (11) 229   (12) 238
(13) 656 passengers (14) 155 extra life jackets
(15) 584 first-time passengers

Answer Key

Day 61: (1) 362   (2) 396   (3) 143   (4) 227
(5) 545   (6) 175   (7) 87   (8) 443
(9) 170   (10) 345   (11) 618   (12) 98
(13) 445 buildings (14) 0 buildings (15) 516 buildings

Day 62: (1) 179   (2) 61   (3) 344   (4) 36
(5) 297   (6) 120   (7) 547   (8) 328
(9) 563   (10) 251   (11) 409   (12) 149
(13) 47 babies (14) 339 girls (15) 651 babies

Day 63: (1) 372   (2) 236   (3) 38   (4) 154
(5) 253   (6) 349   (7) 57   (8) 69
(9) 584   (10) 518   (11) 262   (12) 81
(13) 205 coins (14) 479 coins (15) 76 coins

Day 64: (1) 385   (2) 278   (3) 553   (4) 283
(5) 305   (6) 96   (7) 168   (8) 74
(9) 436   (10) 641   (11) 429   (12) 317
(13) 187 points (14) 166 points (15) 353 points

Day 65: (1) 2,399   (2) 2,480   (3) 3,995
(4) 4,786   (5) 2,154   (6) 726
(7) 47,554   (8) 6,553
(9) 5,693 files (10) 2,866 files

Day 66: (1) 5,789   (2) 271   (3) 949
(4) 1,429   (5) 798   (6) 5,004
(7) 85,904   (8) 27,139
(9) 48,708 people (10) 679 tickets

Day 67: (1) 686   (2) 1,753   (3) 2,758
(4) 2,838   (5) 3,868   (6) 3,074
(7) 12,041   (8) 4,335
(9) 1,768 years (10) 595 images

Day 68: (1) 2,408   (2) 2,313   (3) 5,877
(4) 2,562   (5) 2,243   (6) 153
(7) 38,927   (8) 3,908
(9) 68,004 sheets (10) 74,644 sheets

Day 69: (1) 7,818   (2) 2,725   (3) 4,018
(4) 6,387   (5) 2,967   (6) 1,080
(7) 23,949   (8) 42,449
(9) 3,850 fireworks (10) 9,112 people

Day 70: (1) 2,843   (2) 5,899   (3) 569
(4) 716   (5) 2,935   (6) 1,041
(7) 18,258   (8) 18,098
(9) 6,528 pieces (10) 9,639 pieces

Day 71: (1) 4,392   (2) 1,727   (3) 3,087
(4) 5,826   (5) 2,637   (6) 893
(7) 33,646   (8) 77,416
(9) 4,157 pictures (10) 2,185 students

Day 72: (1) 4,414   (2) 878   (3) 4,780
(4) 255   (5) 2,232   (6) 678
(7) 54,899   (8) 10,517
(9) 6,604 people (10) 4,753 people

Day 73: (1) 482   (2) 4,734   (3) 2,606
(4) 479   (5) 2,632   (6) 4,455
(7) 7,901   (8) 25,406
(9) 1,758 emails (10) 189 emails

Day 74: (1) 3,392   (2) 3,955   (3) 2,371
(4) 573   (5) 8,269   (6) 4,455
(7) 37,431   (8) 56,288
(9) 1,463 people (10) 677 hot dogs

Day 75: (1) 115   (2) 59   (3) 178   (4) 875
(5) 192   (6) 26   (7) 910   (8) 186
(9) 416   (10) 126   (11) 788   (12) 26
(13) 9 meters (14) 122 sharks (15) 88 minutes

Day 76: (1) 55   (2) 195   (3) 833   (4) 37
(5) 622   (6) 142   (7) 464   (8) 1497
(9) 60   (10) 459   (11) 550   (12) 132
(13) 627 people (14) 319 skiers (15) 161 hot chocolate drinkers

Day 77: (1) 48   (2) 149   (3) 178   (4) 1,581
(5) 532   (6) 461   (7) 146   (8) 641
(9) 215   (10) 39   (11) 845   (12) 76
(13) 325 beads (14) 39 beads (15) 221 beads

Day 78: (1) 1,195   (2) 486   (3) 725   (4) 17
(5) 235   (6) 666   (7) 1,935   (8) 24
(9) 522   (10) 75   (11) 27   (12) 1,211
(13) 1,103 fish (14) 373 more gold fish (15) 485 gold fish

Day 79: (1) 562   (2) 1,635   (3) 754   (4) 521
(5) 1,539   (6) 445   (7) 67   (8) 1,250
(9) 1,115   (10) 90   (11) 1   (12) 609
(13) 116 more sea lions (14) 88 sea lions (15) 327 sea lions

Day 80: (1) 275   (2) 1,176   (3) 741   (4) 640
(5) 265   (6) 281   (7) 62   (8) 1,257
(9) 651   (10) 856   (11) 124   (12) 164
(13) 515 apples (14) 13 apples (15) 78 apples

Answer Key

Day 81: (1) 84 (2) 416 (3) 924 (4) 737
(5) 750 (6) 423 (7) 1171 (8) 603
(9) 624 (10) 415 (11) 964 (12) 961
(13) 686 people (14) 194 non-surfers (15) 755 people

Day 82: (1) 148 (2) 1635 (3) 1,016 (4) 149
(5) 354 (6) 1,461 (7) 317 (8) 479
(9) 932 (10) 1,281 (11) 535 (12) 352
(13) 1,517 cards (14) 173 cards (15) 1,088 cards

Day 83: (1) 62 (2) 447 (3) 244 (4) 17
(5) 1,002 (6) 821 (7) 445 (8) 165
(9) 1,365 (10) 236 (11) 436 (12) 258
(13) 1,183 pages (14) 946 pages (15) 237 pages

Day 84: (1) 427 (2) 862 (3) 946 (4) 308
(5) 913 (6) 1,626 (7) 72 (8) 257
(9) 412 (10) 1,071 (11) 610 (12) 411
(13) 320 flowers (14) 26 flowers (15) 137 flowers

Day 85: (1) 1,072 (2) 91 (3) 687 (4) 1121
(5) 36 (6) 900 (7) 189 (8) 1,444
(9) 93 (10) 1199 (11) 485 (12) 660
(13) 172 vehicles (14) 35 vehicles (15) 531 vehicles

Day 86: (1) 188 (2) 1,335 (3) 136 (4) 931
(5) 61 (6) 702 (7) 842 (8) 548
(9) 266 (10) 1,638 (11) 821 (12) 629
(13) 1,718 letters (14) 206 letters (15) 173 letters

Day 87: (1) 483 (2) 710 (3) 307 (4) 1,354
(5) 1001 (6) 19 (7) 51 (8) 907
(9) 259 (10) 832 (11) 250 (12) 246
(13) 62 years (14) 73 years (15) 135 years

Day 88: (1) 1297 (2) 123 (3) 956 (4) 371
(5) 61 (6) 155 (7) 1020 (8) 358
(9) 1,731 (10) 663 (11) 48 (12) 1,317
(13) 158 vehicles (14) 278 vehicles (15) 24 minutes

Day 89: (1) 593 (2) 575 (3) 984 (4) 257
(5) 851 (6) 698 (7) 167 (8) 1,665
(9) 65 (10) 455 (11) 961 (12) 761
(13) 931 bees (14) 175 bees (15) 251 bees

Day 90: (1) 703 (2) 19 (3) 538 (4) 645
(5) 681 (6) 324 (7) 285 (8) 957
(9) 558 (10) 804 (11) 161 (12) 762
(13) 255 megabytes (14) 41 megabytes (15) 214 megabytes

Day 91: (1) 764 (2) 367 (3) 196 (4) 904
(5) 72 (6) 371 (7) 969 (8) 817
(9) 49 (10) 1,021 (11) 460 (12) 127
(13) 186 points (14) 12 points (15) 26 points

Day 92: (1) 278 (2) 907 (3) 1142 (4) 337
(5) 853 (6) 38 (7) 665 (8) 1,554
(9) 298 (10) 168 (11) 188 (12) 141
(13) 87 minutes (14) 102 minutes (15) 17 minutes

Day 93: (1) 1,044 (2) 945 (3) 184 (4) 526
(5) 376 (6) 1,097 (7) 1,220 (8) 28
(9) 304 (10) 251 (11) 1,263 (12) 961
(13) 216 items (14) 160 items (15) 16 colored pencils

Day 94: (1) 789 (2) 1,131 (3) 172 (4) 1,507
(5) 467 (6) 1,600 (7) 69 (8) 617
(9) 132 (10) 938 (11) 575 (12) 253
(13) 115 people (14) 69 people (15) 250 cookies

Day 95: (1) 472 (2) 188 (3) 1,313 (4) 68
(5) 160 (6) 1,121 (7) 345 (8) 390
(9) 268 (10) 1,025 (11) 1,204 (12) 291
(13) 415 points (14) 57 points (15) 64 points

Day 96: (1) 346 (2) 1,101 (3) 96 (4) 1167
(5) 1,519 (6) 116 (7) 350 (8) 263
(9) 76 (10) 842 (11) 39 (12) 732
(13) 78 invitations (14) 21 people (15) 141 cards

Day 97: (1) 578 (2) 1,301 (3) 127 (4) 1,174
(5) 556 (6) 1,305 (7) 28 (8) 560
(9) 169 (10) 378 (11) 1,242 (12) 50
(13) 1,551 plants (14) 275 plants (15) 449 plants

Day 98: (1) 1,892 (2) 646 (3) 136 (4) 37
(5) 333 (6) 1,051 (7) 347 (8) 1,463
(9) 601 (10) 717 (11) 344 (12) 265
(13) 685 people (14) 31 votes (15) 83 girls

Day 99: (1) 329 (2) 610 (3) 170 (4) 492
(5) 120 (6) 156 (7) 915 (8) 274
(9) 1,526 (10) 478 (11) 1,526 (12) 77
(13) 464 views (14) 388 views (15) 466 views

Day 100: (1) 294 (2) 292 (3) 504 (4) 1,116
(5) 778 (6) 105 (7) 610 (8) 359
(9) 1,165 (10) 35 (11) 27 (12) 1,214
(13) 282 laps (14) 124 laps (15) 158 laps

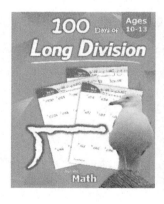

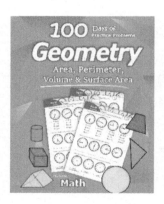

ISBN: 978-1-63578-303-2

Current contact information can be found at:
www.HumbleMath.com
www.LibroStudioLLC.com

Made in the USA
Monee, IL
10 January 2021